Industrial Strength Poems and Short Stories

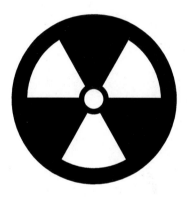

by Larry "Radar" Cada

RoseDog🐾Books

PITTSBURGH, PENNSYLVANIA 15222

ISBN # 0-8059-9390-8
Printed in the United States of America

First Printing

For information or to order additional books, please write:
RoseDog Books
701 Smithfield St.
Pittsburgh, PA 15222
U.S.A.
1-800-834-1803
Or visit our web site and
on-line bookstore at www.rosedogbookstore.com

The author dedicates this book
to his wife and Patience.

To Sheryl
From Larry "Radar" Cado

911

This number conjures up a vision
And on a Tuesday Terrorists struck
The Twin Towers in New York
Ending ours and the Nation's luck.

For never before in our history
Has such a devastation took place
Against our country and its people
By terrorism that we now face.

It was not carried out alone
And the message sent was clear.
They wanted to end our freedom
And all that we hold dear.

So now we engage our enemy
And we unite as a whole.
To hold those that were responsible
For all of the death toll.

The Wall

As I walked toward the wall
I had a sense of insecurity,
That felt like a broken foot
Which brought my mind to reality.

As I saw the many names my worry
Of the unknown disappeared, and
The pain left my stomach. I was
At peace without fear.

Some ignore freedom most their
Lives. It's like happiness until
It's gone. So the wall was the
Same, just as words in a song.

"Freedom's just another word
For nothing left to lose."
Then "The beat goes on."
And death pays our dues.

U.A.W.

As the workday begins
The workers feel relief
For without the U.A.W.
They lose their belief.

It's not just Union dues
That makes our Union strong
Look at all the members
That sings the solidarity song.

The Union was developed
To help out the common man
But throughout all the struggles
It's blessed this great land.

With all the sweat and toil
That the Union had to endure
It's made a lot of workers
Go out and join for sure.

When some U.A.W. Local
Goes out on strike
Other members will participate
That's what it's like.

Just as the U.A.W. symbol shows
With members hand in hand
It shows their support
In this great land.

This goes to show the country
That the Union is here to stay
For without our bargaining unit
We wouldn't have much to say.

Black Lake

Not just a memory
For members to see
It makes you experience
How the Union will be.

It starts with workshops
With every member in mind
So that they'll be trained
In most duties they find.

Their areas are chosen
On the very first day
The time and study
Is what makes it pay.

As the days pass by
The lessons are learned
Making the sisters and brothers
All the more concerned.

When the last day is finished
And graduation is near
They celebrate their victory
With a solidarity cheer.

Walter Reuther

He was a man of greatness
Who was ahead of his time
Fighting for each and everyone's rights
For a fair contract to sign.

He wanted all workers to share
In the fruits of their labor
Because they did the physical work
Which management thought was a favor.

The conditions that they worked for
Weren't the best to be desired.
For the workers didn't have rights
And if they complained were fired.

So he lead the Solidarity crusade
To help workers break their bond
From the way Management would rule
So the old ways would be gone.

Steve Yokich

When the time had finally come
To pick a new U.A.W. leader
The delegates made their best choice
So he could replace Owen Bieber.

The one they chose would work
And make sure that we won.
On almost every issue we tackled
Making sure our work was done.

He didn't know the word defeat
For he just didn't back down.
Helping members take on big Corporations
That's where Union activists are found.

When a crisis finally did come
No matter where the fight was.
You'd find Steve Yokich right there
Because every fight fought, was his cause.

President Ron Gettlefinger

When the swearing-in was over
And Ron Gettelfinger took the chair,
Our future turned a bit brighter
With a President who cares.

He's shown us how to succeed
By helping keep members' jobs secure
So our union will be stronger
So they won't have to fear.

And as for all those Corporations,
They should all hold on tight.
Because Ron's going to knock some over
Fighting for everything that is right.

Let us all say a prayer
That President Ron Gettelfinger leads us,
And protects us from Corporate greed
By raising a little fuss.

Battle of the Overpass

It was just an organizing drive
With leaflets to be passed out
But it soon turned to tragedy
That made the organizers shout.

As Walter Reuther and other members
Went to assemble at gate 4
They walked up to the overpass
To spread their message once more.

When all of a sudden
They were kicked, slugged and beat
By Ford's Service men
Which was a cowardly feat.

With photographers at the scene
All the pictures were taken
To tell of the organizers ordeal
So the victims weren't forsaken

As Time Magazine ran the story
Ford Motor Company denied the fight
This helped to get workers support
To show that the Union was right.

Solidarity Forever

This song is for those who'll listen
And make sure we remember the past.
For to forget all the Union's struggles
Would be an atrocity that shouldn't last.

So every member stand up and recall
How some sisters and brothers were shot.
Trying to make sure their demands were met
Otherwise we wouldn't have what we got.

Everytime contract time starts over again
The Corporations want to take away.
I think of all those factory workers
Who helped make our life a better way.

So as the September deadline draws near
It makes me want to cry.
And also say a few words of respect
For all those workers who had to die.

Open Shop

With just one reason in mind
These companies tend to surface
To make a mockery of labor
For their own personal purpose.

They treat their own workers
With, "You better do what I say"
For if they don't respond
It just might be their last day.

Each working day brings pressure
And a quota to match working
Under strenuous conditions
Just to get out the next batch.

When payday finally arrives
And the workers open their check
The monetary difference is clear
How they sacrifice their neck.

Then there's the seniority worker
Who had twenty-one years but, the
Company had to let go and his job
Fell on fallen ears.

With all the right to work shops
That is located in this state
Those workers should be concerned
They don't wind up outside the gate.

Organizing

Since our membership begin to shrink
And the Corporations failed to hire.
We should all start to organize
Or the United Automobile Worker's could expire.

With our vast network of Locals
And using computers as our tool.
We could speak to the masses
By advertising on the Internet too.

We can explain our reasons why
And show what they can gain.
For with the computer helping us
It would save time to explain.

And after they've made their decision
And our membership starts to climb.
We can thank our dedicated organizers
Who helped save your job and mine.

Time after Time

Workers earned the right at contract time
That we receive our fair share.
For we have sacrificed for years
Now it is time for companies to care.

With the contract being negotiated
Our concessions should be noted.
Showing how much we lost
When all of the members voted.

Then there was the time
That the companies asked for more.
Asked for a two-tier hiring system
Hiring new workers for less at their door.

So it's been time after time
That the companies have cashed in
Now it time to see wage increases
Showing that our Union is strong again.

Tax Abatements

The intent of tax abatements
Was for cities to lend a hand
Giving company's a tax break
To develop on their land.

It wasn't intended for companies
To move away after 10 or 12 years
But, General Motors took advantage
And left Willow Run in tears.

With their plant soon shutting down
Some workers will have no guarantee
About job placements or location
They'll just have to wait and see.

The workforce is the scapegoat
And their future is bleak
No thanks to General Motors
For the new jobs workers seek.

This tragedy should send a message
To all the workers of this State
That tax abatement is a Trojan horse
With promises that are late.

Larry "Radar" Cada
Local 372, U.A.W.

Dayton Hudsons

To stop it's Westland employee's
From keeping their Union vote.
Dayton Hudson's had the courts
Reject it in a note.

With two Republican Judge appointees
On the Appeals Court.
There wasn't much of a chance
The Judges would give their support.

It was the employee's decision
To form their own Union.
But Dayton Hudson's saw it differently
And started all the confusion.

Now the employee's need your support
What if it had happened to you?
Let us prevent this injustice
Let's show them what we can do.

So tell your friends and family
What Dayton Hudson's has done.
Don't shop at Hudson's, Mervyn's or Target

Until the Westland employee's have won.

Made in USA

With all of our country's problems
The one that stands out the most.
Is why American sales are down
From the Atlantic to the Pacific coast.

It's our biggest problem today
Knowing our economy can't compete.
Building a lot of products
Seeing our sales prices beat.

With the Japanese one reason
And Mexico not too far behind.
It provides for a stumbling economy
With lots of solution to find.

Some people say they don't care
Because they save money every day.
Yet what happens when you're unemployed
And your not making any pay.

So when you're standing in line
About to buy yourself that next snack.
Turn around and look at the unemployed
Whose futures are under attack.

Job Security

It's not to be taken lightly
For it protects every workers right
To invest in his everyday labor
To retire someday without a fight.

If this resolution would be adopted
So that jobs could be protected
It would be the best solution
Ending downsizing which has been neglected.

The Corporations have supported cutbacks
That reduced our current workforce.
Which made it very difficult
Delivering production quotas on course.

So, I hope this resolution passes
And gives our membership some relief.
So we don't have to worry
Helping to end this awful grief.

Outsourcing

Thoughout the history of labor
There's never been this much gloom
That outsourcing has caused the workers
Who want to end this awful doom.

Their jobs are threatened everyday
By the companies outsourcing of parts
And replaced by foreign labor
Showing profits on their charts.

When will this injustice stop?
So those millions will not suffer
With the loss of their jobs
That will make their lives tougher.

The time for action is now
To send all companies a demand
That they leave our livelihood alone
In this great land.

So when contract time comes around
And outsourcing is put on trial
Make sure that it is cremated
And put its ashes in a pile.

Dual Sourcing

It's just a way for Corporations
To make our demands sour.
By having sought another source
To prevent our bargaining power.

With a second factory with parts
They wouldn't listen to us speak.
They could continue with their business
While we were out on the street.

So just try to imagine
Coming to work one day
Seeing the padlock on the factory
Remember you said "no way."

It can happen just this way
If we don't face the fact
And start right away to organize
Or we won't have time to act.

Downsizing

With only half of the work force
The factory work is being done.
Sending a vital message to America
Downsizing needs to be undone.

By eliminating most of its workers
Putting our livelihood at risk.
Causing us to work overtime
Making safety a factor on our list.

It doubled up our work in
Both production and skilled trades
We need more help in all areas
So that this atrocity will fade.

So the only way downsizing will vanish
Will be with every workers unity
To make all the companies listen
And stand up to their responsibility.

Profit Sharing

It was put into the contract
So we could get our share.
For helping DaimlerChrysler to profit,
Making it our business to care.

When the first payment was paid
And the quality began to rise.
Sending a message to our stockholders,
Sharing profits with worker is wise.

The Corporation has made the effort
And paid the fruits of our labor.
It has helped to strengthen morale,
Putting our trust in their favor.

So let us as a team
Continue to embrace this great plan.
So that we can all prosper
Working as partners hand in hand.

Unification

As our calendar year winds down
And we face the year 1999.
Most of the Unions face reductions
Which threaten your job and mine.

We must now begin to act
Making sure Unification is our goal.
So, members, become strong in numbers
Making sure all Corporations know.

Uniting the U.A.W., Steel and Machinist Unions
Would help strengthen our bargaining power.
So we could have the edge
Making it the Union's finest hour.

So, let us send a message
Making sure Corporations read our lips
That Unification is our ideal solution
To release us from their grips.

Larry "Radar" Cada
Local 372, U.A.W.

Unity

It's not a very long word
But with lots of Union support.
It grows to make us strong
With lots of solutions to sort.

With each of us standing firm
And holding each and everyone's hand.
There's nothing that we can't accomplish
When every member takes a stand.

They'll be times that seem impossible
But unity will keep us strong.
So that the American Labor Movement
Will keep our support rolling along.

So when those Corporations who scoff
And say the Union will lose.
Just remember that it's member unity
Every Union's member's going to choose.

Full Cola on Pensions

Let us all make a motion
One that needs to be done.
By adopting full COLA on Pensions
So that justice can be won.

As every worker does their job
They've made the Corporation's profit more
Now it is time to send
A full COLA to our door.

With all the profits Corporations make
Full COLA would be a trickle.
Compared to the Chairman's yearly salary
It'd be hardly worth a nickel.

So we must now all unite
Bringing full COLA to the bargaining floor.
So everyone's future will be secure
Helping kick fixed income out the door.

Cola on Pensions in 2003

If we don't support COLA on pensions
Making it the number one contract demand.
The retirees will be denied the security
For which to live and survive in this land.

Some workers will say it'll never happen
Because the cost would be too great.
But take a look at the Congressmen
Who collect COLA after their retirement date.

Then there are the U.A.W. International Solidarity House Reps
Who qualify for COLA when they leave
This justifies that the retirees
Get the same benefits that they receive.

So contact your delegates to the National
Bargaining Convention telling them to
Make COLA the number one demand.
And ask them to pledge their support
To give the retirees a helping hand.

Scabs

Let us drive these offenders away
The ones we know as scabs.
For they take away jobs
And put them up for grabs.

The main reason that they surface
Is to break the Union's back.
By doing the employers bidding
And distorting all the facts.

The learned how to intimidate,
Coerce and permanently replace
Many of today's striking workers
Who lose their jobs and their case.

It's not a pretty sight
For the workers to be in.
Losing their jobs because of scabs
It must be a sin.

The next time you have a chance
Tell your neighbor or a friend
About the plight of the workers
So that this injustice may end

Caterpillar

Its just a greedy company
That wants the Union busted
Their methods of intimidation
Prove they shouldn't be trusted.

The current contract has ended
But the company won't negotiate
This leaves all the employees
With their jobs to contemplate.

When last years strike ended
With no sign of relief
The U.A.W. told the employees
Hold on to your belief.

To make the company notice
That the Union was serious
They started a slow down
Which made them delirious.

With its workers moral dwindling
Caterpillar is sure to back down
This will show the American public
That the Union won the last round.

Larry "Radar" Cada
Local 372, U.A.W.

True Lies

Caterpillars paying of Union officials
Wasn't written in gold
So they stopped paying them,
Putting their futures on hold.

It wasn't the first time
That Caterpillar tried a charade
By making the National Relations Board
Believe the Union should fade.

The rejection of the contract
Was the start of Caterpillars crusade
To try and eliminate the Union
Which found their heart mislaid.

So let us all take a vow
To stop Caterpillar's true lies
By telling all the American people
It's the Union that they despise.

True Colors

It seems the Detroit News wouldn't bargain
To give their Employees their share
And now they have finally committed
To firing them without a care.

It's just as if they planned
From the beginning not to agree
To any of the Union's proposals
Showing their true colors for all to see.

With the New Year upon us
And the Employees without a prayer
This should show the Michigan people
They now need somebody to care.

So the next time you approach
That News or Free Press stand
Do the Employees Family a favor
By keeping your money in your hand.

Walk on By

When you see a Detroit Free Press,
News or USA newsstands make
Sure you walk on by. Don't
Purchase their Scab paper, then
Go tell everyone why.

When all was said and done
The Union thought the contract
Fair. Only to have the company
Say that some workers couldn't
Be there.

The company started a lock out
And the Union had to agree,
Or the jobs those workers held
Simply would not be.

There can be a happy ending
If everyone would help support
All those newspaper workers
By not buying Gannett papers of any sort.

An Injury to One

The Detroit Newspaper Strike isn't over yet
Which the company won't let demands be met.
For its employees who want justice won
To bring its scab total to none.

From the start of the strike
The Company was prepared to fight
For the company had its scabs in place
Which really didn't make it right.

Every Union member should take heed
Whenever there is "An Injury to One."
Every brother and sister could be next
Solidarity in many is much better than none.

So the next time you have a chance
To help with their cause or plan.
To get their jobs back with pay
Tell everybody to boycott where they possibly can.

No Scab Paper

There shouldn't be any reason
Why any scab paper is brought.
By any union auto worker
Stopping the striker's cause to be fought.

Just put yourself in the strikers shoes
With no paycheck for any week
So that they can't pay their bills
It's only a fair contract they seek.

If you want to read a paper
Choose one that is not on strike.
One that treats their employees with respect
An honest paper which everyone would like.

So tell everyone "No Scab Paper"
And victory will be around the bend,
Helping to win the battle
So that the striking workers will win.

A Clear and Present Danger

As I come to work everyday
To help my company do it's best.
I've heard that its all for nothing
Because NAFTA has failed the test.

When is our Government going to pass
A North American Free Trade Agreement that's fair
So Americans won't lose their jobs
And have somebody that will finally care.

We know there's big money involved
So that many Corporations will profit.
But it cuts away the workers job
With hardly a way to stop it.

Everyone should pick up his or her pen
And write to stop this loss of American Labor.
So tell your Congressman and Senator
To pass an Amendment in our favor.

Farewell to Don Lingar

As Don Lingar's job comes to an end
It was Local 372's big loss.
He helped us to get engines
And he got his ideas across.

When the membership needed education classes
He made sure our needs were met.
So that we could educate ourselves
Making our goals easier to get.

When the Local contract was up
And the company wanted the M.O.A.
Don told them no to Outsourcing
Or that it would be DOA

So this poem is dedicated to Don Lingar
A three term President who did succeed.
To make all the best decisions
Always thinking of our needs.

NAACP

Its the oldest civil rights organization
That has lasted throughout the years.
Still maintaining its goal of helping
To free mankind of racial fears.

The year it began was 1909
To stop the lynching of Negroes
Then it began to help others
To end all they're racial woes.

Just as the initials stand for
Its NAACP
Which is the National Association For
The Advancement Of Colored People.
For all the world to see.

The leader who guides this Association
President Kweisi Mfume is his name.
Who's doing the best job possible
Keeping all the goals the same.

Slick Willy

One man had the nerve
To enter the presidential race
Only to have his background
Slandered in his face.

They called him Slick Willy
And put him down
But he ran in the election
Never making a sound.

The word was soon out
That he had an affair.
But his wife had forgiven him
And the people didn't care.

They questioned his leadership
And the progress of his state
Only to make him angry
But it was too late.

As the election day came
And the people started to vote
The results favored Clinton
And Bush put on his coat.

Election 92

The time has come
For Clinton and Gore
So they can kick
Bush out the door.

It hasn't been easy
These last four years
Paying high taxes
And shedding our tears.

We're taking back America
With President Clinton's aid,
So we can stop worrying and
Let our troubles fade.

No more lips to read
Only Clinton and Gore
To make our country strong
And help the poor.

It's been worth every minute
Voting George out the door
With God and conscience
We couldn't stand four more.

Clinton and Gore

The time has come
To re-elect Clinton and Gore,
To keep our economy growing
By taking control once more.

We don't need voodoo economics
That the Republicans once used,
To scare the American people
Showing Government was misused.

What we still need in office
Is Bill Clinton and Al Gore,
So all the work they've done
Won't be swept out the door.

So when Election Day is here
Tell your family and friends why,
You're voting for Bill and Al.
So the American Dream won't die.

Election 96

This Election had two good Candidates
Two men who had different views.
Who to vote for wasn't that difficult
Because everyone had lots to lose.

Clinton was the first in the Election
To show what he stood for.
And the people gave their support
To him and Vice President Gore.

Dole was running a close second
And he just couldn't keep up.
For everything that he promised people
They told themselves it wasn't enough.

When the Election was finally over
President Bill Clinton won four more years.
To build bridges to the 21st Century
Leaving Dole to cry "96" Tears.

Election 2000

If ever there was a decision
That put our livelihood at risk.
Which of the Candidates to choose
Should be high on our list?

As we look over their credentials
And see what they have done.
We finally come to a conclusion
That our trust should be won.

When we enter the voting booth
And cast our vote for President.
Experience should be on our minds,
So we'll have a message sent.

And then we'll analyze the Candidates
Deciding our choice is Al Gore
For he meets all the criteria
By helping everyone even the poor.

Say A Little Prayer

Now that the Election is over
Let every one of us unite.
So we all have a future
That's promising and bright.

We should not let the past
Dictate how our future should be.
There should be a new beginning
To strengthen our Union's Solidarity.

Let our bygones be bygones
And put them to rest.
So everyone can start over
Putting our leaders to the test.

Let us all say a prayer
That all our leaders help us
And lead us through the future
Showing America it's Unionism we trust.

Safety Lockout

There shouldn't be any reason
Why a Tradesman doesn't lock out
Any and all Safety Lockout devices
Helping eliminate accidents without a doubt.

It only takes a few seconds
To snap the lock in place
So that you'll be well protected
From your feet to your face.

So let all Tradesman take action
And shut down this awful danger
By practicing Safety Lockout procedure
Which will make fatalities a stranger.

When all the accidents are counted
We're sure to see a decrease
Because we practiced Safety Lockout
Which made most plant injury's cease.

Safety Equipment

In today's work environment we labor
Not realizing what we could lose.
When it comes to sight and hearing
Every one of us should follow the rules.

Just a piece of metal
Broken off from a machined part
Could leave a worker without vision
And future to a bad start.

Even our hearing should be protected
Because of the noise we hear
For if we don't protect ourselves
No sounds will come to our ear.

So just as in Las Vegas
We don't want our luck gone
Let's win the big jackpot
By keeping our Safety Equipment on.

Safety Awareness

With the start of the working day
I look at my hands and feet.
Always feeling its fortunate
They're still there, no thanks to
Close calls that they meet.

It doesn't take a genius to
Realize it's luck that saves the
Day. For many a careless worker
Taking chances where dangers lay.

By practicing safety awareness we
Give workers the right guarantee.
So when an unsafe hazard exists
They won't become victims, you see.

Now when you start your jobs make
An effort to spot. Any and all
Close dangers so they'll be
Eliminated, and you not.

Shaft Alignment

It really doesn't take very much
To throw a machines alignment out.
But when this critical situation happens
Its time that it's realigned throughout.

There's several methods that are mainly used
To correct the misalignment that we see.
Among them is one called rough alignment
Having a steady hand is the key.

The rim and face follow this
Which reads more accurate then the last.
But still leaves something to be desired
Even though this method isn't as fast.

The next one is the reverse indicator
Which has two indicators to match.
Both are checked for bar sag, making sure
Their knobs are tightened so it doesn't detach.

The most expensive of all the methods
Is the one that's called the Laser Shaft.
It shoots a beam of laser light
Making it a state of the Art Craft.

But the one that is the most effective
That most of the Alignment experts have found.
Is the reverse indicator alignment method
Which shows that it is the best around.

Vibration Analysis

Its a cost savings program
That has reduced the downtime.
So that companies don't waste money
Which put products on line.

With the advance in Technologies
It was a sure win.
By detecting vibration in machines
So that corrections could begin.

From the data base collecting
To transducers that you mount.
The information was compiled correctly
So that its credibility would count.

Its also called Predictive Maintenance
Which tracks imbalance and phase.
And predicts and finds errors
Showing industry that it pays.

Millwrights

There's never a day that doesn't go by
Some Millwright work has to be done.
To chain, pulley or drive coupling
Making sure that the lines run.

When the assignments are handed out
The last thing that's on their mind
Is how the job will be done?
Because they don't know what they'll find.

From the job on the assembly line
To a department that they support
Every repair is made with precision
Giving each one a satisfactory report.

They fix the job the first time
So they don't have to return.
So that the factory can make production
Making job security their main concern.

Pipefitters

If it wasn't for the Pipefitters
The various departments could not run
For they maintain pumps and pipes
So different operations can be done.

All the pits have several pumps
That pump coolant to a machine
Keeping its fixtures and tooling cool
It's where quality can be seen.

If the pumps do not operate
We have to shut production down
That's where the Pipefitters come in
Because they're the best in town.

So next time you're working
And another product goes out the door
Take another look at your check
That's where the Pipefitters made you score.

Machine Repair

Whenever the machines start having problems
Machine Repair is sent in.
To make sure that they're repaired
Before production can start to begin.

They must have lots of knowledge
On how all the parts turn.
So that they're all taken apart
And fixed before they can return.

There are times they have to climb
To get to the broken part
So they can untighten the bolts
Having the bad station taken apart.

As they start their final assembly
You can see their skillful work.
For which the parts are assembled
Making sure the bolts has torque.

Tinsmiths

This job takes plenty of concentration
For it involves lots of bend.
So that different thickness of metal
Will line up with it ends.

It involves knowing a lot of geometry
So you get your angles straight.
For if it's laid out wrong
The parts will never mate.

It's a trade that demands accuracy
So all the parts fit.
Giving us good protection
Protecting us from objects that hit.

Whenever you see the Tinsmiths working
You know it's for our cause.
They're helping to protect our livelihood
By being there whenever safety calls.

Toolmakers

When machines needs some parts made
So that the operation will run
You can depend on the Toolmakers
To make sure it gets done.

The whole operation is taken apart
And new parts made without haste.
So that it does away with downtime
And also does away with waste.

Sometimes it involves a little part
But without it, machines can't run.
So without our crew of Toolmakers
All the repairs would remain undone.

So whenever I pass a Machine
I feel good, Toolmakers are here.
Helping to protect our Job Security
Because I know that they care.

Electricians

This job requires lots of respect,
For they're always on the alert
Working with high voltages everyday
Making sure they don't get hurt.

It's not just wiring up circuits
Because it involves troubleshooting most days
So that the machines start up
And run in all the bays.

It requires a lot of training,
To become a Skilled Trades Electrician.
But when the training is over,
The hard work has just begun.

So whenever you start your machine,
Just remember who wired it up.
So that it could finally run
Making sure your job isn't rough.

Oilers

Whenever some machines start to leak bad
There's only a handful to be found.
But if it wasn't for the oilers
The machines wouldn't make a sound.

It's the oil that they put in
That keeps all the bearing turning around.
So that the part can be machined
Helping to keep the factory's losses down.

It's their dedication to their oiling job
And making sure machines are always filled
That keeps our counts up
Where we can have something to build.

So when your machine starts to leak
And the pressure starts to fail
It's the oilers that are called
So this story has a happy tale.

Hi-Low Drivers

Not a job too big
Not a job too small
For the drivers to handle
Always being on call.

Some days are simple
Other days are hard
But it doesn't matter
Because they're always on guard.

Their job is to deliver
And I've seen them move
It's all in their timing
Like a needle in a groove.

They'll handle any problem
That's thrown their way
Because nothings too hard
That's what makes it pay.

They get our product on line
And everyday it shows.
By moving the parts on time
Which the whole plant knows.

Janitors

When the time comes
And the job is no fun
You can depend on the janitors
To get the job done.

There's more that meets the eye
It's all in a working day
With hard strenuous work
But they make it pay.

With numerous duties to attend
From using a Hotsy steamer
That gets rid of dirt and oil
And makes the plant cleaner.

Sometimes in a moments notice
A department has a spill
Only to notify the janitors
That it needs their skill.

With all this hard work
It's a wonder how they last
After one job is done
They start on another task.

Good Housekeeping

Whenever a tour comes to Trenton
The company has every janitor perform.
Their duty of scraping and cleaning
Bringing all violations back to norm.

But when the tour is over
And the Corporate Officials go home.
The Company reduces the janitors overtime
Causing all their efforts to roam.

It doesn't make very much sense
To bring Good Housekeeping to pare.
And then shut down most cleaning
Eliminating everything janitors did so far.

So let us all ask Corporate
Why the janitors cannot maintain
The weekly cleaning of this plant?
So their integrity will be the same.

Absenteeism

What makes this problem so important?
It puts quality in the hole
By not having properly trained employees
That reduces each and everyone's goal.

That goal is to improve our quality
So that our product can be sold
To keep everyone at our plant working
Or else it'll be forced to fold.

Everyone should start by doing his or her part
To come to work every scheduled day
And help to keep our jobs safe
By getting absenteeism out of the way.

Just remember the next time you miss
You're not the only person that's involved
It also affects each and everyone's livelihood
So make sure this problem is resolved.

Attendance

Let us all ask a question
About the fate of our lives.
Does it take a full crew
To assemble, or don't we realize?

If we worked for another company
We just wouldn't pick and choose
When to show up for work
In the end we would lose.

The last time that I looked
Everyone here was on my team
To give their support every day
That's the way it should seem.

So when you answer this question
Do it with an open heart so that
You'll protect everyone's job
Bringing attendance to a good start.

Liberty

Whenever I look at a coin
There's a word that I see
And it has exactly seven letters
Which spells out the word Liberty.

I know it's taken for granted
By some Americans, young and old.
But to me it means freedom
In the belief that I hold.

Just as in our country's Constitution
Its " Liberty and justice for all."
Which should make us all proud
Having everyone of us stand tall.

So whenever you count your change
Take a look in your hand
And see what protects our heritage
Showing its Liberty in our land.

Peace

As I wake up every morning
The first thing I think of
Is that I'm very blessed
Living in peace like a dove.

Some country's are not so lucky
For war is their main menu
And the dead is their plate
Showing that quarrels are to continue.

Our country learned their lesson early
By adopting certain basic principle rights
So we could have our freedom
By which we eliminated most fights.

I'm not saying that we're perfect
But until there's another lesson plan
I'm glad to be an American
Living in peace in this land.

Being an American

It's that first breath that we take
That sets us aside from all others
For we're blessed with God given rights
The same as our fathers and mothers.

From the very first word we spoke
To everything that we will ever learn.
Our gratitude goes out to our forefathers
Whose freedom of speech was a main concern.

As each of us started to crawl
And then we learned how to walk
We all started to witness our freedom
And we all had good reason to talk

For it set wheels of liberty in motion
And it made everyone around the world see
That we're the melting pot of all denominations
By being an American it makes us free.

The Flag Still Stands For Freedom

As I look at our flag
I notice how proud it waves.
The ideals that it stands for
And the dignity that it saves.

It always did stand for freedom
Through all the years it flew.
With all the changes of styling
Sent a message that was true.

And now with our country's problems
We need it more than ever.
To help us get through war
That we triumph in our endeavor.

So now we face this challenge
Sending a message that is clear.
That our flag stands for freedom
Helping protect everything that is dear.

God Bless America

If there was anyone more fortunate
To bless this country of ours,
And which us stand beside her
In the wars and bleakest hours.

Then I'd say it was God
Who has given us his blessings,
And made sure that we survive
With the bible and his lessons.

"From the mountains, to the prairies,
"To the oceans," and sky above,
God has chosen to bless everyone
With his almighty devotion of love.

Whenever we look to the heavens
We are sure he's always there,
Blessing us and our great country
Showing everyone that he does care.

Don't Tread On Me

This country don't take idle threats
And terrorists know how we feel.
If they mess with our democracy
Bad consequences are their next deal.

Our nation is joined by freedom
And a strength that's seldom seen.
But when it is finally shown
The world knows what we mean.

To prove that we have freedom
And it's a right that's given.
Take a look at other countries
With the conditions that they're living.

Then turn around and praise God
For helping each and everyone,
And saying, "Don't tread on me."
Making sure our work is done.

Star Spangled Banner

Since our flag changed over time
It's been flow with great pride.
Showing it brightest stars on earth
Letting our freedom be our guide.

Its displayed on ever flag pole
To let the whole world know.
That its the, "Star Spangled Banner,"
Making our pledge of allegiance grow.

Whenever our country had to defend
They called a charge for victory.
Leading all our military to glory
Which gave respect for our history.

So let us pray to Jesus Christ
"For the land of the free,"
"And the home of the brave,"
Protecting America as it should be.

America the Beautiful

As I look upon America
I see a country that's free
From the west to the east
For each of us to see.

You can travel in any direction
The signs will be the same.
Painted a bright green and white
With every state emblem and name.

As you travel down the highway
You'll see the well-trimmed grass.
On either side of the pavement
Whenever the other cars go pass.

And as you approach your exit
And leave the expressway far behind.
You'll always love, 'America the beautiful"
With all the adventures you find.

In God We Trust

As I look out upon America
I can see why we're free.
To do the things we do
So it protects you and me.

It starts out with our belief.
Which states "In God We Trust."
Making sure our right to freedom
Isn't violated and that its just.

Even through our present day life
There's opposition to end our right.
To keep, "In God We Trust"
Being printed and out of sight.

So let's protect our democratic right
To keep those words we seek
"In God We Trust", we raise our flag
To keep our freedom complete.

Proud to be an American

Let us all give our thanks
To our country at every grace.
Being proud to be an American
With every challenge that we face.

We should all count our blessings
To our country as a whole.
For if we didn't live here
We couldn't let our patriotism show.

Whenever the "Star Spangled Banner," plays
And the last word is sung.
Our pride is shown with attention
Wherever the American flag is hung.

So let us all make a promise
To the almighty Lord up above.
That we'll always defend this country
Being proud and showing our love.

Jan Jarvis

We know that she's in heaven
For she did so much good.
By helping all of God's children
Sharing all the love she could.

So now the drum is silent
And everyone should not weep.
For we've lost a great friend
Who's memories we'll always keep.

As we look to the future
We shall always remember her smile
And know that she's at peace
Because her life was worth while.

She was a great lady
And now that she is gone.
She is in everyone's thoughts
From every dusk through dawn.

Written By Larry "Radar" Cada and James Fields

Jesus Christ

We put our trust in Jesus
And hope our life works out
Only to find some problems
That makes us holler and shout.

If only we had more faith
And practice what we preach
The world would be a better place
For all the sinners we would reach.

It would help us to say a prayer
For a relative or a friend.
This would be a start for salvation
So that religion would not end.

The world is made up of religions
From which you are free to choose.
All you which to do is pick one
So you don't have to lose.

The next time you are angry
Don't take it our on your fellow man.
Put your trust in Jesus Christ
And give him a helping hand

Sharing

There's times that I've often wondered
How better our world would be?
If everyone of us would share
A greeting to you and me.

There's just not enough of love
To give to our fellow man.
Until our life is in trouble.
Then we all lend a hand.

I know we're all gods children
And not sharing should not be.
For we're put on this earth
To do Gods work you see.

Let us all make a promise
To say a prayer at grace.
To share with one and all
Having a better world to face.

Left Behind

One day millions of believers disappeared
And the rest were "left behind."
Carried away by an overwhelming emotion
That brought happiness to their mind.

Then there came the wicked Anti-Christ
Who filled the world with distress
And denied and opposed Jesus Christ
As all his actions would confess.

As the Anti-Christ spread his evil
And everyone around him looked displeased
There came the Second Coming of Christ
Which brought Anti-Christ to his knees.

So the Anti-Christ fate had come
And was conquered forever by Christ
Never to fill the world with wickedness
And "left behind" was the Anti-Christ.

Tribulation

With the rapture in full swing
They were those that wanted saved
So they started a "Tribulation Force"
Telling those "Left Behind" to behave.

They would meet with each other
And they would ask the reason why
Each of them were "Left Behind"
And after each session they would cry.

Their plan was to be ready
So when Judgment day finally came
That each of them received Jesus
And their motives were the same.

But then the Anti-Christ appeared again
And tried to stop their plan
Then he was met with the Lord's prayer
Making him vanish from the land.

The Wrath of the Lamb

It was the rise of the AntiChrist
And Nicolae Carpathia was his name
Who won people's trust and confidence
Showing that the first Judgment came.

For from the start, trouble began
Giving everyone four reasons to worry.
The Four Horsemen of Apocalypse
Just became their Judge and Jury.

So the second Judgment to strike
The one that was called War
Took some of the believers by surprise
Which brought death to their door.

The third Judgment was Famine and Plagues
Which caused some of the population to be gone.
Which was eliminated by its force
Showing what was left at dawn.

The fourth one was called Death
Which was more severe than before.
For it almost broke the believer's spirit
But the Lord said no more.

And the sixth Judgment did come
Then "The Wrath of the Lamb" did appear.
Causing a great earthquake to move the earth
Which Jesus sent a message that was clear.

Assassins

It was foretold in a prophecy
That four murders would take place.
And one would be the antichrist
Who gets hit in the face.

The first murder to take place
Was Pontifex Maximus Peter the priest
Who was injected with a virus
Because of orders from the beast.

So it was the next two
Of the murders to take place
As Carpathia grabbed Eli and Moishe
Shooting at their neck and face.

The two witnesses met their fate
As the antichrist emptied his gun
Into their bodies as everyone saw
The evil deed that was done.

Next the antichrist approached the crowd
Showing them his eyes of red
But before his hands dropped down
A sword hurtled toward his head.

So the fourth murder had come
And proved the prophecy was true.
But then the resurrection took place
And the antichrist arose good as new.

King of the Abyss

Its written in the Holy Bible
The King of abyss shall appear.
To lead demon locusts on rampage
So unbelievers would be in fear.

The sky was black as pitch
And the racket deafening to ears.
As the creatures attacked the unbelievers
Leaving the believers without any fears.

From the smoke came flying creatures
The color of yellow and brown.
Miniature horses with tails like scorpions
Attacking the unbelievers on the ground.

Unbelievers lay writhing, screaming and thrashing
Slapping at their body and knees.
Also trying to cover their face
And they called out saying , please.

Most of the unbelievers were stung
They each would ask to die.
And would suffer for five months
Then escaped death and asked why?

So the fifth trumpet judgment had come
Making sure the unbelievers would see.
That the Lord was a forgiving God
And that salvation was the key.

Soul Harvest

Without so much as a warning
The earthquakes pushed the earth aside.
Causing most of the believers to separate
Making most find shelter to hide.

Then the believers started to dig
And they struggled on their knees.
By each searching high and low
With hopes to find their families.

When the earthquakes finally did stop
The believers began their daily quest.
To search for truth and life
And put the devastation to rest.

Then there came a great multitude
For which no one could foresee.
And put their trust in Jesus
For all of mankind to see.

Love

It starts out so very quickly
With a message to the brain.
That something has upset your rhythm
Telling you it's time to explain.

With all your systems on hold
You try to imagine their name.
Only to find out it's dangerous
To avoid it leads to pain.

Then the bow is strung back
And the arrow is let go.
Only to have your heart pound
Thinking your lover has said no.

But when it's finally over
And you've chosen your mate.
It's love that has wings
And has sealed your fate.

Don't Let My Love Fade

There are times of trials and tribulations
That has set my love astray.
For it has made it fade
And someday I'll have to pay.

Why don't I open my eyes?
And let the truth come in.
So I can save my love
Before all the consequences begin.

I can stop this cruel affair
And put my life on track.
By promising to renew my love
And giving my true love back.

So just stand by my side
And help me to give you.
That love that almost faded
So my love can be true.

Muscles & Fatigue

The day starts off quite early
With certain jobs to do
Making it hard on certain muscles
That does the work for you.

As you look at your assignment
Your muscles start to fatigue
Sending messages to your brain
Asking to join another league.

It doesn't matter that you're tired
For the company depends on you
To build your best product
For the entire world to see.

Just when your muscles start to give
And the pain starts to climb
You make sure that you deliver
All the parts on time.

So its muscles and fatigue
That builds your livelihood
And shows the entire whole world
That all your products are good.

Ground Hog

He's been compared to a thermometer
And he's not made of glass.
He's usually right about the weather
By predicting when winter will pass.

The towns folk let him sleep
Almost all of the whole year.
But when February 2 does arrive
They wake him with a loud cheer.

He goes about his weather business
By sniffing the cold winter air.
Then looks down on the ground
Hoping his shadow isn't there.

The town where he lives at
It's not a very big place.
But when Punxsutawney Phil sees his shadow
You should see everyone's unhappy face.

Humming Bird

As they flap their wings together
With all the speed, they can.
They give out strong vibrations
Creating a sound like a fan.

Then as they lose their altitude
And pollinate flowers as they land.
You can see it s nature s function
Reproducing without the hand of man.

As they start their upward flight
Their wings are beating real fast.
For they are our natures helicopter
For them, it s an easy task.

Whenever I see a Humming bird
I know their heart is true.
For they help our flowers bloom
Making life beautiful just for you.

Barracuda

The name brings up a vision
Of a car that had speed.
And showed all the American people
Chrysler muscle cars took the lead.

For also in the ocean deep
There eventually came a real threat.
For all of the Scuba divers
That the deep-water barracuda met.

So both barracuda's picked up speed
And looked somewhat liked the same.
For you didn't wanna be there
Because you didn't wanna feel pain.

The one took the quarter mile
By blowing smoke through its headers.
And the other sliced the water
Making all the Scuba divers bettors.

So they both served their purpose
And left their page in history.
And made sure that we noticed
Those winners are not a mystery.

Turtle

When anyone mentions the turtles name
They know it rhymes with hurdle.
For it's been a proven record
Races are lost as a turtle.

We've all seen the famous race
The one with the turtle and hare.
And saw the hare run fact
While the turtle just stood there.

But just as in real life
The turtle doesn't want to lose
And starts to forge a plan
To give the hare his dues.

With the help of his family
The turtle stationed them every mile.
So the hare thinks its him
Who's already been there awhile.

But the hare doesn't wanna lose
And then starts his mad dash.
Only to spot the lone turtle
On the finish line holding the cash.

To The Editor

Whenever you have something to say
Write it down in a letter
And send it to your paper
Expressing your opinions, ideas, or whatever.

It could be something about work
That you want an answer for
So don't delay for a minute
Send your question "To the Editor."

There's always room for a poem
Or maybe an article from you
That could be about Union struggles
Or any other important subjects, too.

So the next time you have a question
Make sure that you send it in
Because there's no such thing as
A stupid question but without
A Question, an answer can't begin.

Patience

Whenever your job gets you down
And your patience is cut thin.
Try and pray to Jesus Christ
Asking for his blessings to begin.

For when he starts to speak
And tells you what to do
Everything that was making you mad
Will vanish, going away from you.

Then you can tackle your job
And see everything that's clear again.
With Jesus's almighty blessing around you
There's no problem you couldn't win.

So as the hours go by
And your patience been built up,
Helping get you through the day
Showing you that Jesus said enough.

The Rainmaker

Everyday someone's deeds always goes unnoticed
By most of us in life.
It's only that when we're threatened
That wakes us like a knife.

It isn't a very pretty picture
For our futures to be in.
To lose all form of tranquillity
The law saying we can't win.

So now we need a friend
One that is thick and thin.
Beyond a benefit of a doubt
Making sure that we can win.

I'm speaking of no other than
"The Rainmaker" who is without fault
Their only objective is to win
So that your misery will halt.

Mother

Her talents are taken for granted
Which show what she can do.
When in most of the situations
Most men wouldn't know how too.

As the day is started early
She gets the breakfast done fast.
Then makes sure everyone's property dressed
From the first to the last.

Then sends everyone on their way
And she gets ready to clean.
All the fixtures in the house
So that everything there will gleam.

Next she cooks the evening meal
And makes sure her family's feed.
For she's earned the title "Mother"
And she's special her family said.

Grandfather

My parents always treat me nice
And always ask me to behave
So when the weekends come around
I can see my Grandfather wave.

I love my Grandfather very much
He always hugs and tickles me.
Telling me how great I am
For he's the best you see.

Sometimes I just can't visit him
And it makes me very sad
But he calls on the phone
And then it makes me glad.

So all you Grand kids listen up
I'm telling you to be good.
So you can see your Grandfather
When he comes to your neighborhood.

Forgotten

She was just nine
Crying on a table
All but forgotten
Like in a fable,

It was Christmas 1905
Not a gift in sight
Dressed in tattered clothes
Waiting for the night.

She fell fast asleep
Hoping someone would care.
The hours past by
But nobody was there.

The same thing happens
In our present time
Lots of poor children
Don't even have a dime.

With poverty and hunger
Throughout this vast land
Let's send out a message
To give a helping hand.

Then dig into your pockets
To help these girls and boys
To have a nice Christmas
With food and toys.

So when you see the Charities
Collecting in the streets
Give money for the children
So that they may eat.

Clothe-A-Child

In the year 1984 at Trenton Engine
A program was devised
To help some poor children
Through their poor lives.

With the aid of management
And the help of its employee's
They pooled their moneys
To give the children some toys.

The plan that was proposed
Was to have a party imposed
At Chryslers Trenton Engine
And have the children clothed.

Now early one morning
The children started to gather
They were offered cookies and milk
And the hunger didn't matter.

The children were then loaded
On a bus headed for Sears
And the sounds of singing
Could be heard by everyone's ears.

Next the sponsors helped the children
Fit into a set of clothes
It was such a sight to see
All the happiness in a pose.

Then it was off to a farmhouse
To hang up some gloves
Upon a Christmas tree
To show their love.

It was back to Trenton Engine
To have the children eat
And after they ate dinner
The tour was the next treat.

Off they went through the plant
Their eyes were astounded by the view
With all their smiling faces
Each of them saying "Thank you."

Now was the time to receive their gifts
Santa Clause and Big Bird were there
Each child in Santa's lap
Knowing some one did care.

After all the presents were handed out
And no one was missed
The Clothe-A-Child committee
Started to make out next year's list.

Future Planning

Everyone should enroll in Future Planning
For it explains how to retire.
So you gain insight and understanding
Giving you security that you desire.

The day that you should start
Is the day you were hired.
For it doesn't hurt to plan
Certain matters before you're retired.

There's information that you should know
That will help you to satisfy.
Any questions that you would ask
Telling you the answers and why.

So you can end the mystery
And sign up for a class.
And let it broaden your future
So that your finances will last.

StayWell

It starts with your diet
By choosing the right meal
So that it eliminates Cholesterol
Giving you the best deal.

Everyone should make an effort
To see that they care
About their body and fitness
Making heart disease rare.

As the months go by
And you record the results
You can see the difference
When they take your pulse.

When you reach your goal
And begin to feel swell
You can start to smile
Because you joined StayWell.

Rumors

They are often told to confuse
And distort all the facts.
By giving workers the wrong impression
That they're getting the ax.

Rumors usually start by unconfirmed information
That begins to trickle in.
But after that starts the fabrication
Causing lie after lie to spin.

It's always by word of mouth
Without even a bit of proof.
Knowing that it's just not true
Causing worry under everyone's roof.

So, we can end these rumors
And put them to rest.
By not paying any attention
And removing the pest.

The Heat is on

In this age of car sales
The heat has been turned on.
Allowing only the strongest to survive
For the weakest will be gone.

It would be to our advantage
To make every effort to perform.
We must now improve our quality
And take the critics by storm.

From the biggest boss at Corporate
To the workers on the floor.
We have to get full cooperation
If we want to profit more.

So tell all your fellow workers
That we're all making a pledge.
To sell all of our products
So we can have the edge.

Neon

This car of the future
That has everybody's attention
Has made Motor Trend Magazine
With lots of styling to mention.

It just wasn't made overnight
It was conceived quite carefully
So the public would be pleased
Making it a good buy economically.

Even before it went up for sale
The orders started to rush in
To buy this bargain item
With the stroke of a pen.

So if you're looking for a deal
The car to get is the Neon
One of the lowest priced models
And it's wonderful to be on.

Trenton Engine Quality.Com

Let us type in this message
So we can get on line.
And make sure customers are satisfied
With Trenton's… Engines…all the time.

For if we improve our quality
And show that we're the best.
All our future sales will follow
Showing we're better than the rest.

I know we can get better
And punch all the right keys.
By keeping a good attendance record
And making sure that we please.

So let us send a message
Showing where Product Quality Improvement belongs.
So that our quality goes up
Making sure that nothing is wrong.

Trenton Engine

It's built more than 30 million engines
And at one time had a sign.
That said it built the best engines
In the world you could find.

But that's not the real reason
That Trenton has survived so long.
Just take a look at performance
Which P.Q.I. and M.O.A. brought along.

The bottom line is the employees
Who have endured the hard years
And built the company to greatness
Which helped eliminate all their fears.

So they know that they're proud
To be part of this team.
That helped bring about its success
By the supporting the P.Q.I. and M.O.A. theme.

Quality

Let me tell you a story
That is both old and new.
About all United States workers
Who's knowledge grew.

They learned about Quality
And the right way to build
A lot of new products
So their orders could be filled.

Their job was inspecting
And they did it with ease.
No needless rejecting
With their expertise.

If some product approached
With a part shy.
The reject button was pressed
So they wouldn't get by.

After the Product moved on
They knew they were right
Quality became a standard
For every Product in sight.

Let it be said
When this story is told
It takes every employee
To have their product sold.

Turnstiles

The Corporation says its cost effective
By keeping track of everyone's hours.
But it's a violation of M.O.A.
By timing every minute of ours.

The contract says no time cards
But what do we have here?
A sophisticated device that tracks us
Causing every one of us to fear.

It's just not the time device
That makes everyone of us mad.
It's being herd through the gates
Like cattle making everyone here sad.

So we should all stick together
And tell our President to object.
By him writing to the Corporation
Telling them those turnstiles we reject.

Sweet Dreams

There doesn't seem to be an answer
To our Country's present state,
For most people just question
Others just turn to hate.

With all of our commitments
That is spread very thin,
It makes me often wonder
If our generation will win.

As changes are flashed by
That upset our daily life,
Which affect everyones children
And cuts like a knife.

Just ask yourself this question
Will you be here tomorrow?
When you're sweet dreams are gone
Or will you be in sorrow?

If I'm Not Happy

There's times of trails and tribulations
That which made my happiness go
There were times I wasn't happy
Acting joyful so it won't show.

As the world is a stage
I made an attempt to hide
My sorrowful disposition not telling why
Hoping truth would take my side.

Along came my reason for cause
For it would set me free
It all came in a rhyme
So that every one could see.

It started out so very simple
If I'm not happy, I'm not happy
And to the hell with joy
Because sadness made me an unhappy boy.

Iacocca

Not just a figurehead
That saved the day
For Chrysler Corporation
And made it pay.

He's did his duty
Just as he saw fit
And made sure that
Our cars didn't sit.

With his world car idea's
He pushed for the mini van
Which sold like hot cakes
In this great land.

To upgrade the Corporation's position
He formulated a plan
To build a new headquarters
All on one piece of land.

It cost the Corporation plenty
But provided lots of space
It made the American people
Aware of our new face.

Next he approved the new cars
The Concorde, Intrepid and Vision
The public liked the styling
And it was a great decision.

With his car commercials
That talked of being a hit
It sold more vehicles
That we could get.

With all his goals reached
Its time for him to go
He's helped us survive
As everybody knows.

Holey O's

It was late at night
When I just settled down
For a big bowl of cereal
And my face turned a frown.

For in my cereal bowl
To my dissatisfaction
There were tiny maggots
That met their attraction.

The maggots were using the O's
For little life preservers.
Swimming in the milk
Like they were on maneuvers.

I then dropped the bowl
And started to choke
Ran in the bathroom
Started yelling for my folks.

My wife wasn't home
And my son was in his bedroom.
I yelled for him
To get me an excedrin.

Every nerve in my body
Was going through pain.
I looked in the mirror
To see if I was the same.

I leaned over the toilet
And decided to heave
In hope that the little ones
Would be sure to leave.

It worked like a charm
And the worms started to exit
My stomach was empty
It was a form of rejection.

Some words to the wise
Always look in those bowls
Or there might be flies
Hiding in those holes.

No Sweat

Whenever the temperature starts to rise
We may start to feel sick.
It's best we begin some precautions
There's always a few to pick.

The first is to drink water
At least eight glasses a day.
So that it guards against dehydration
Cooling your body temperature this way.

Next wear light colored clothing
For it lessens the heat you get.
Making your body feel a lot cooler
So that it reduces your time to sweat.

So whenever summer heat arrives
Make sure that you don't feel regret.
Just follow these simple precautions
So you can say "No Sweat."

Faith

Lets not be afraid of anything
When there's no way to turn.
Face it and turn to faith
Helping your heart and soul return

Then take some time to pray
For when faith is with us.
There's nothing that we can't do
Helping keep our belief and trust.

And as our life continues on
And most of our troubles fade.
We can thank the Lord almighty
For all the right decisions made.

By making sure we have faith
It will save our very soul.
It's with our Lords own blessing
Showing everyone the path to go.

The Great Depression

Throughout the history of time
There was a lot of gloom.
The great depression caused the people
Who wanted to end its awful doom.

With the shutting down of factories
It caused the economy to slow.
Which made people lose their jobs
And have no place to go.

The soup kitchens helped to feed
Some of the people on the street.
But lots of others who were hungry
Didn't have a chance to eat.

When a job would be open
Thousands would come to apply.
Even if it was for a few openings
They gave it their best try.

It lasted throughout all the thirties
Which was the longest in time.
That the people had to suffer
Where a fortune was a dime.

So time had made a decision
Which our government couldn't resolve.
Until the new deal had surfaced
Making the great depression revolve.

Leon's Family Dining
Lincoln Park

You won't find another fine restaurant
That has your family in mind.
Providing you with lots of choices
Of meals you will find.

The daily specials you can't beat
For the value of the meal.
It's one of the lowest priced
Which gives you the best deal.

All the employees at the restaurant
And that goes for Sammy too.
Have only one goal in mind
And that's to always serve you.

So whenever you get the urge
To have a home cooked meal.
Come over to Leon's Family Dining
Because satisfaction is what you'll feel.

Written By Larry 'Radar" Cada & Rose Ann Kemeny

It's A Beautiful Day

Here at Trenton Engine you need not go far
To run into Larry our "Radar"
Walking down the aisle with tools in tow
Comes the man we all know
Headed to the job with a shuffling step
Always pleasant and full of pep
As he passes he makes our day brighter
Lifting our spirits making them lighter
This is the reason Mr. Cada can say
Without a doubt "It's a beautiful day"

Written by Mark Lemerand about me.

Bye Bye Blackbird

It was the 5th of September and I had just arrived home from work when my wife ran out of the house screaming bloody murder. What could have happened to her? I kept asking myself. She was acting like she had just taken the early pregnancy test and we had tested positive. This wasn't the case. What really happened was that a Blackbird had flew down our chimney and landed in the kitchen. It became apparent that my wife was scared of birds. I wasn't too thrilled about birds either. When I was younger, a robin flew down and pecked me on the head, so I was afraid too.

Through the kitchen window I could see a small dark figure hovering over the dining room table. It seemed to be giving out Morse code with its wings, one wing up, one wing down, ten up again. I could make it out because I had taken Morse code in the Army. It said, "Don't try it buster." This bird was going to get caught, it was just a matter of time. My son and I devised a plan to catch the bird. We were to get dressed up with blankets over our bodies, put on goggles, gloves, and wrap towels around our heads. This would protect us from any harm the bird would infect us, or so I thought.

The moment my son and I stepped into the kitchen dressed up like the "Stars Wars, Sand People," the bird started to notice us. He looked one way and then another. Next he started to fly within a few feet of us. I told my son to arm himself with a broom and I would grab a mop handle. When the bird started his next advance towards us we were able to charge him. "Bang, Kapow," these were the sounds that were coming from the kitchen. If someone had been passing by they would of thought that the TV program BatMan was on. Just then he landed on the hole in the wall room divider in the living room and was making ugly faces at us. My son went into the living Room and I stayed in the kitchen so he could not escape. When the time was right I threw my mop handle at the bird and my son did the same with the broom. Both of these weapons hit him on the head. This was it, the moment of decision. What would he do? His pupils in his eyes were becoming dilated. It was just too much in one day for him. Well, as anyone can see, our day wasn't going too good either. How many times a year do you get a visit by a blackbird? Just then the blackbird swooped down, grabbed my towel with his beck and started flying away, I could feel the pressure around me. My ears started to hurt. This was starting to get to me. There was only one solution to this problem. Both my son and I were to have Blackbird for supper. We were both mad as hell. This bird, this flying chicken who invaded our home would soon feel our wrath. What diabolic plot did we have in mind? There was only one. When the blackbird landed next time I would put a container of salt on his tail. I heard that by doing this it would stop a bird from flying, or was it just a couple of grams of salt on the tail?

The Blackbird stopped flying and landed on the floor. Now was my chance. I hurried and put some salt on his tail. The moment I did this he started to flip over. It was too much for him. I told my son that this should be a lesson for him. It takes more than brute force to catch your enemy, it takes a skillful plan.

The Gold Dollar

My best friend had invited my wife and me to a bar to see some Go Go dancers. The bar was called the Gold Dollar, and it was located in Detroit. I had no reason to believe it was not a strip joint. My wife's mother was to go with my friend as a blind date. As we entered the front door everything looked like a normal bar should look like. It had a couple of Go Go girls with real skimpy g-strings, they were shaking their bodies all over the stage. Right away I noticed this real cute blond with a fantastic smile and big kahoonas. They were as big as the Twin Towers of Fermi II at Monroe, Michigan. They seemed to be sending out a kind of vibration as they swung to and fro. My wife started to notice that I was paying too much attention to the stage and none to her. This was it, was I a man or mouse? I drove the family car so it was narrowed down to that I was a man.

"Honeybun I said, there is no other girl for me." Just about that time a car backfired and it sounded like the Battle of the Bulge. I jumped on the floor thinking that we were under attack by some unknown force. Finally I jumped to my feet and sat down so no one noticed what I did.

The blond that I was looking at walked by my table and winked at me. The whole table started to shake, she had struck a nerve, I was in love. Moments later she started towards the Ladies' room, I followed in hot pursuit. The area by the Ladies' room was empty so I decided to go to the mens' room in the mean time. As soon as I entered the mens' room a small slender figure of women was standing next to a urinal taking a leak. Was I really seeing this or was it my imagination? It was the same blond that was dancing at the bar. Here I was in the mens' room with a morphadite, half man, and half women. The only way for me not to be seen was to keep my mouth shut. Every muscle in my body froze until he or she left. When I got back to my friends at the table everyone wanted to know where I had been. I told them about my experience in the mens' room. Everyone blamed me for my lack of self-control.

My wife and I hadn't been getting along and this kind of shock might be just the medicine she deserved. Well, it wasn't she hauled off and hit me with her purse. It hurt like the dickens. If you ever been hit with one you'll know what I mean. It's about the same as when somebody steps on a roach except worse. It just goes to show what happens to a husband who starts to backslide from his marriage. How was I to know it was a guy, I don't have twenty twenty vision?

Just then all of us saw the blond kissing another girl with his big red lips. It finally dawned on us that we were in a gay bar just like in the Blue Oyster on Police Academy. After that all you could see were four flashes and signs of smoke speeding through the front door. It was unbelievable, we all ran the 2 Minute mile to the parking lot. When I returned home I must have taken about 10 showers to make sure nothing was infected on me. As I look back on that day, I justify the visit by saying "You can't judge a book by its cover."

Holey O's

Let me tell you about the time one November night when my wife wasn't home and I was all alone. I hadn't eaten dinner and I was awful hungry. I usually just ate some cereal until my wife came home. I went to the cupboard and took the Holey O's box and poured myself a large bowl of the little O's. I put a lot of milk and two giant spoonfuls of sugar in it. I like my cereal sweet so I don't have to taste the oats in it. Then I went and sat down on the couch to eat. While I was eating, I saw something move in the Bowl. Was I seeing things? I had been eating with the lights turned off, watching Television. I took my spoon and moved the Holey O's apart in the bowl. Within seconds a little head with a white body and one black eye was looking at me. I said, "Oh my God, What has happened to me, I'm poisoned." I had just eaten one bowl and started on my second one. It was almost finished when this occurred. My stomach started to feel queasy. I thought, what did I eat? I turned on the lights and took a closer look into the bowl. There in the bowl were about twenty baby fruitflys or what looked like maggots using the Holey O's for life preservers. I wanted to vomit. I had just eaten almost two bowls of the little creatures. Now I was feeling the after effects.

I picked up the phone and called the emergency ward at the hospital and asked for poison control, They told me to wait a minute. I had just swallowed a considerable amount of fruitflys and asked what was I to do about it. They said just to wait until my bowel's moved. Well, I said since I ate the fruitflys everything's been moving except my bowels. They also suggested I throw up. Well, I was never very good at doing that. I talked to a Doctor who must have thought he was Ben Casey because he told me just to watch some Television and let nature take its course. The Doctor said," Why are you getting excited over just eating a bunch of protein? "I said, "Look doc, how would you like to have a dozen future flies making home in your stomach?" To me, I had not invited the little guests, after all you can't screen all the cereal on the market. I then asked to talk to a Specialist. They said they would have to fly one in. I said, "That's the reason I'm in trouble." If you need some flys, I have plenty. Finally, I just hung up the phone.

The bathroom was the only solution to my problem. I had to get rid of the little pests. I went into the bathroom knelt before the toilet, opened my mouth and stuck my biggest finger down my throat. It was like a volcano eruption. I started to choke and gag. The fruit started to fly. I mean everywhere. I hadn't done this before. I don't recommend it to anyone. The O's were flying everywhere, up, down, on top of the toilet, on the mirror. It was like an Atomic Plant melting down, I was on Ground zero. The only place to be was in the next room. After I was depositing the remains of my meal to points known and unknown, I cleaned the room. I counted about 200 Holey O's everywhere.

I went back into the kitchen to the scene of the crime. To me, there was a crime committed. The first thing I did was to read the top of the cereal box for the expiration date. I couldn't find the date, it was torn apart. I think that's why the manufactures put the date on top because of experience like mine. I was looking for evidence that would link them to some liability. There are only two situations. One being that the cereal box was more than five years old or how else could the maggots have got into the Holey O's. The other would be that the maggots were transported in the box from the factory, from the grocery store and then to my house. I was Playing Colombo but odds were stacked against me. What court in this land would take my word against a Multi-Million-Dollar Corporation. I had eaten the evidence and all my Complaints are here say. A few words to the wise, the next time anyone approaches a bowl of cereal, take caution learn from my lesson eat only flat flakes.